PASSING THE TIME
Entertainment in the 1800s

DAILY LIFE IN AMERICA IN THE 1800s

PASSING THE TIME
Entertainment in the 1800s

by
Zachary Chastain

Mason Crest Publishers

MASON CREST PUBLISHERS INC.
370 Reed Road
Broomall, Pennsylvania 19008
(866)MCP-BOOK (toll free)
www.masoncrest.com

First Printing
9 8 7 6 5 4 3 2 1

Library of Congress Cataloging-in-Publication Data

Chastain, Zachary.
 Passing the time : entertainment in the 1800s / by Zachary Chastain.
    p. cm. — (Daily life in America in the 1800s)
 ISBN 978-1-4222-1785-6 (hardcover)   ISBN (series) 978-1-4222-1774-0
 ISBN 978-1-4222-1858-7 (paperback)   ISBN (pbk series) 978-1-4222-1847-1
 1. Amusements—United States—History—19th century—Juvenile literature.
 2. Entertainment events—United States—History—19th century—Juvenile
 literature. 3. United States—Social life and customs—19th century—Juvenile
 literature. 4. Community life—United States—History—19th century—Juvenile
 literature. I. Title.
 GV53.C39 2011
 790.097309034—dc22
                              2010022264

Produced by Harding House Publishing Service, Inc.
www.hardinghousepages.com
Interior Design by MK Bassett-Harvey.
Cover design by Torque Advertising + Design.
Printed in USA by Bang Printing.

Contents

Introduction

History can too often seem a parade of distant figures whose lives have no connection to our own. It need not be this way, for if we explore the history of the games people play, the food they eat, the ways they transport themselves, how they worship and go to war—activities common to all generations—we close the gap between past and present. Since the 1960s, historians have learned vast amounts about daily life in earlier periods. This superb series brings us the fruits of that research, thereby making meaningful the lives of those who have gone before.

The authors' vivid, fascinating descriptions invite young readers to journey into a past that is simultaneously strange and familiar. The 1800s were different, but, because they experienced the beginnings of the same baffling modernity were are still dealing with today, they are also similar. This was the moment when millennia of agrarian existence gave way to a new urban, industrial era. Many of the things we take for granted, such as speed of transportation and communication, bewildered those who were the first to behold the steam train and the telegraph. Young readers will be interested to learn that growing up then was no less confusing and difficult then than it is now, that people were no more in agreement on matters of religion, marriage, and family then than they are now.

We are still working through the problems of modernity, such as environmental degradation, that people in the nineteenth century experienced for the first time. Because they met the challenges with admirable ingenuity, we can learn much from them. They left behind a treasure trove of alternative living arrangements, cultures, entertainments, technologies, even diets that are even more relevant today. Students cannot help but be intrigued, not just by the technological ingenuity of those times, but by the courage of people who forged new frontiers, experimented with ideas and social arrangements. They will be surprised by the degree to which young people were engaged in the great events of the time, and how women joined men in the great adventures of the day.

When history is viewed, as it is here, from the bottom up, it becomes clear just how much modern America owes to the genius of ordinary people, to the labor of slaves and immigrants, to women as well as men, to both young people and adults. Focused on home and family life, books in this series provide insight into how much of history is made within the intimate spaces of private life rather than in the remote precincts of public power. The 1800s were the era of the self-made man and women, but also of the self-made communities. The past offers us a plethora of heroes and heroines together with examples of extraordinary collective action from the Underground Railway to the creation of the American trade union movement. There is scarcely an immigrant or ethic organization in America today that does not trace its origins to the nineteenth century.

This series is exceptionally well illustrated. Students will be fascinated by the images of both rural and urban life; and they will be able to find people their own age in these marvelous depictions of play as well as work. History is best when it engages our imagination, draws us out of our own time into another era, allowing us to return to the present with new perspectives on ourselves. My first engagement with the history of daily life came in sixth grade when my teacher, Mrs. Polster, had us do special projects on the history of the nearby Erie Canal. For the first time, history became real to me. It has remained my passion and my compass ever since.

The value of this series is that it opens up a dialogue with a past that is by no means dead and gone but lives on in every dimension of our daily lives. When history texts focus exclusively on political events, they invariably produce a sense of distance. This series creates the opposite effect by encouraging students to see themselves in the flow of history. In revealing the degree to which people in the past made their own history, students are encouraged to imagine themselves as being history-makers in their own right. The realization that history is not something apart from ourselves, a parade that passes us by, but rather an ongoing pageant in which we are all participants, is both exhilarating and liberating, one that connects our present not just with the past but also to a future we are responsible for shaping.

—Dr. John Gillis, Rutgers University
Professor of History Emeritus

1800 1801 1803 1804

1800 The Library of Congress is established.

1801 Thomas Jefferson is elected as the third President of the United States.

1803 Louisiana Purchase—The United States purchases land from France and begins westward exploration.

1804 Journey of Lewis and Clark—Lewis and Clark lead a team of explorers westward to the Columbia River in Oregon.

1825 1838 1839 1841

1825 The Erie Canal is completed—This allows direct transportation between the Great Lakes and the Atlantic Ocean.

1838 Trail of Tears—General Winfield Scott and 7,000 troops force Cherokees to walk from Georgia to a reservation set up for them in Oklahoma (nearly 1,000 miles). Around 4,000 Native Americans die during the journey.

1839 The first camera is patented by Louis Daguerre.

1841 P.T. Barnum opens Barnum's American Museum in New York City, where he shows oddities from around the world, many of them staged acts.

1812

1812 War of 1812—Fought between the United States and the United Kingdom.

1814

1814 Francis Scott Key writes the poem from which the lyrics for "The Star Spangled Banner" are taken.

1820

1820 Missouri Compromise—Agreement passes between pro-slavery and abolitionist groups, stating that all the Louisiana Purchase territory north of the southern boundary of Missouri (except for Missouri) will be free states, and the territory south of that line will be slave.

1823

1823 Monroe Doctrine—States that any efforts made by Europe to colonize or interfere with land owned by the United States will be viewed as aggression and require military intervention.

1843

1843 The Virginia Minstrels, widely credited with the creation of minstrel shows, appear in New York City.

1844

1844 First public telegraph line in the world is opened—between Baltimore and Washington.

1848

1848 Seneca Falls Convention—Feminist convention held for women's suffrage and equal legal rights.

1848(-58) California Gold Rush—Over 300,000 people flock to California in search of gold.

1854

1854 Kansas-Nebraska Act—States that each new state entering the country will decide for themselves whether or not to allow slavery. This goes directly against the terms agreed upon in the Missouri Compromise of 1820.

1861

1861(-65) Civil War —Fought between the Union and Confederate states.

1862

1862 Emancipation Proclamation— Lincoln states that all slaves in Union states are to be freed.

1864

1864 Central Park Zoo opens in New York City.

1865

1865 Thirteenth Amendment to the United States Constitution— Officially abolishes slavery across the country.

1865 President Abraham Lincoln is assassinated on April 15.

Time Line

1876

1876 Alexander Graham Bell invents the telephone.

1878

1878 Thomas Edison patents the phonograph on February 19.

1878 Thomas Edison invents the light bulb on October 22.

1881

1881 Annie Oakley wins a shooting match against Frank Butler, her soon-to-be husband, marking the beginning of her career as an entertainer and marksman.

1883

1883 Bill Cody founds his "Buffalo Bill's Wild West" show in Nebraska.

1867

1867 United States purchases Alaska from Russia.

1869

1869 Trans-continental Railroad completed on May 10.

1870

1870 Fifteenth Amendment to the United States Constitution—Prohibits any citizen from being denied to vote based on their "race, color, or previous condition of servitude."

1870 Christmas is declared a national holiday.

1871

1871 P.T. Barnum first organizes his traveling circus and freak show, which would grow to become what Barnum billed as "The Greatest Show on Earth."

of the 1000s

1890

1890 Wounded Knee Massacre—Last battle in the American Indian Wars.

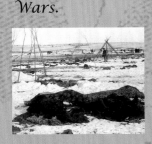

1892

1892 Ellis Island is opened to receive immigrants coming into New York.

1896

1896 Plessy vs. Ferguson—Supreme Court case that rules that racial segregation is legal as long as accommodations are kept equal.

1896 Henry Ford builds his first combustion-powered vehicle, which he names the Ford Quadricycle.

1898

1898 The Spanish-American War—The United States gains control of Cuba, Puerto Rico, and the Philippines.

1899

1899 Scott Joplin releases his song "Maple Leaf Rag" and quickly becomes a famed and influential ragtime composer.

Part I:
Practical Delights

Work and Play

When you think about entertainment today, a thousand distractions come to mind: video games, DVDs, online gambling, board games, amusement parks, roller skating rinks, movies, iPods, and more all vie for our attention. Finding something to do, some way to entertain oneself, is never a challenge in twenty-first-century America.

Now try and imagine a different landscape, one not so crowded with advertisements and eye-grabbing colors. Imagine the noise of TV commercials fading away and being replaced by the steady thud of an axe into wood, or oxen grunting under the weight of a plow. America in the early 1800s was not only missing modern technology, it was missing cities and suburbs too. Yes, a few urban centers existed in the early 1800s—Philadelphia and New York being the largest—but for the most part, America was rural. People worked the land for their livelihood. If you wanted

This nineteenth-century painting shows an entire New England community harvesting cranberries. The ladies have obviously worn their best hats for the occasion!

to eat, you had to grow food. Work took up a huge portion of people's every day lives. Blankets had to be sewn, cows milked, chickens fed, crops planted, laundry scrubbed by hand. To live was to work hard.

It makes sense, then, that much of the entertainment in those days was a way to make work pass more easily. If you had to shuck corn, you might as well make a game of it, or do it in mixed groups, so that young men and women could meet and flirt with one another. In fact, this is exactly what many rural Americans did in the 1800s—they made games of work.

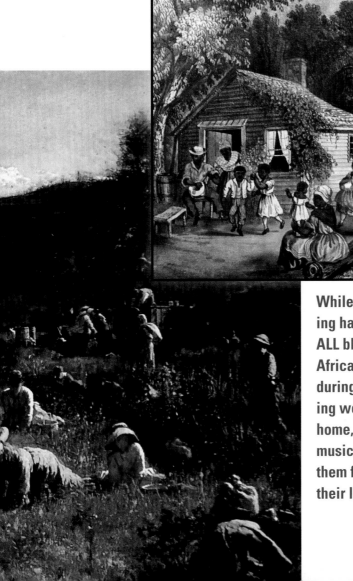

While most white families were working hard during the nineteenth-century, ALL black families were as well. African Americans' only entertainments during this time were found either during work or in the privacy of their own home, where the heritage of dance and music their ancestors had brought with them from Africa continued to enrich their lives.

Harvest Time

One of the most basic forms of "passing the time" at work was the shared harvest. During harvest time, farm families and their neighbors took turns going from farm to farm to lend a hand. Although very little of the work they did could be called "light," the expression, "Many hands make light work," expresses the philosophy of the day. By themselves, a single family might take weeks to finish the harvest, but with the help of friends and neighbors, the work could be done in days. Very rarely if ever did families keep records of "who helped who" or for how long. It was more common for people to give help where it was needed, until the work was done—and they could expect the same in return.

Sharing the harvest was not just practical, it was fun. While picking crops by hand, harvesters could talk, laugh, and share news. With the exception of babies and very small children, harvest time included everyone. Even the youngest

Harvest time involved entire families. The hard physical work could be overlooked in the pleasure of getting together with friends.

children, who had very little to offer by way of work, provided entertainment to the adults. Over time, the American harvest encouraged the creation of many work-games. Some were competitive, the most famous being the corn-husking competitions that have lasted right into the present day.

Corn Husking and Shucking

The processing of corn for either animal or human food was hard work. After the corn was harvested, the leaves and corn silk had to be removed from each individual ear of corn in a process called corn husking or shucking.

A corn-husking contest was a competition, usually between men, to decide who could shuck the most corn by hand in a given time frame. Some contests lasted all day, others only an hour or two. In the 1800s, some men gained local or regional fame for being able to husk corn at incredible speeds. Scores were kept by keeping track of how many bushels of corn each man shucked.

EYEWITNESS ACCOUNT

J. D. Calhoun of the *Lincoln Weekly Herald* on December 3, 1892, reminisced about his "valuable and romantic experience as a corn shucker." Calhoun, a former homesteader in Franklin County, recalled:

I farmed and raised corn, and shucked it, and hired other men to shuck. We once hired one of those 100 bushels [per day] men and at noon he hauled up a consumptive looking load of stuff—with shucks sticking out of it like feathers on a ruffled pigeon—that might measure but could not weigh out 25 bushels. At night he would come in after dark with the same kind of a yield of his labor. He spent the evening around our hospitable fireside, telling how it was the hardest corn to shuck he ever saw, and how he had knocked out 100 bushels in a day for [neighbor] Dave Plasters the fall before. We let him go and got another man who held the championship belt of Atchison county, Mo. . . . He shucked 60 bushels one day and then laid up for repairs with mutton tallow [for the blisters on his hands].

Barn Raising

Another example of work-related fun was the barn raising. A barn raising is just what it sounds like—neighbors gathering together to build (or "raise up") a barn. Barns were an essential part of rural life, especially in the colder climates of North America. A barn was a necessity for storing hay and keeping animals, and it usually needed to be built as soon as the family's house was standing. Sometimes, more than one family shared a single barn.

The process of raising a barn had a very organized structure. The older folks who had raised many barns in their day took "crew chief" positions, and younger folks took their instructions. Women were expected to provide food, water, and other necessities, while the men worked on the building itself. Meanwhile, children gathered to watch, learn, and occasionally lend a hand by carrying tools to workers. All in all, it was a time for the entire community to gather together and have fun while important work was done. Barn raisings were anticipated with excitement. Men competed for certain skilled jobs, and children looked on with envy, wanting to join the fun (but difficult) work.

As this late nineteenth-century photograph shows, the entire community—men, women, and children—turned out for a barn raising.

Quilting

A "quilting" was a gathering of women to make a quilt. Today, many quilts serve a purely decorative purpose (meaning they are hung on walls or placed on display instead of used for bedding), but in the 1800s, these were practical and well-used pieces of bedding. Women gathered in circles for "quilting bees" to share fabric and designs, and often to work on a single quilt together. A quilting was the perfect time to exchange news, tell stories, and share laughter while a quilt was created by the group's joint effort. Sometimes quiltings were turned into competitions, and teams worked together to finish a quilt before the other competitors.

This quilt made in the 1840s reveals the ways in which a quilt could serve to express women's creativity, faith, and industry, all at the same time. A quilt was a piece of art—but it was not intended to be hung on a wall; instead, it would keep someone warm on a cold winter's night.

Church in Rural Communities

The church was the center for social life in rural communities. Far from being a place only to worship and listen to sermons, the church was where people could meet and talk without making plans. Just as many people today use cafes, gyms, and parks to meet friends or strangers, the church was used as a way to meet and talk without an appointment. The Sunday morning church service may have sometimes been less than ideal for social purposes, but people made do with what they had.

Sometimes the church sponsored a more casual event called a "church social." The church social was often organized around a meal. Sometimes this was a "potluck" meal in which everyone brought a dish to share. Other times it was an outdoor picnic. Some

churches even formed sports teams or put on dances. Later in the century, rural churches were keenly aware of the temptations of city life and the many entertainments to be found there. They tried to offer a few amusements of their own, enough to keep children away from what older people saw as the more dangerous attractions of the city.

Camp meetings—outdoor religious gatherings, usually held in the summer—were times of spiritual renewal, but they were also exciting times of social activity and entertainment for rural farmers in the 1800s.

Church in Urban Communities

In the cities, churches realized that they were only one of many options for entertainment. There were amusement parks, restaurants, pool halls, and saloons to contend with. The church tried to compete as best it could, trying different ways to entertain its young people, many of which involved food. Food (most of it, at least) was not controversial, nor did it lead any young people astray!

Urban churches benefited greatly from the waves of immigrants that

Church socials in more urban areas became very exciting events, with fancy decorations, lots of food, and a general party atmosphere.

The church was the central hub of African American social life during the 1800s.

arrived in the 1800s. The church was especially good at helping immigrant communities hold on to their native cultures. It preserved language by offering services in the immigrants' native tongue and brought people together to socialize around meals made from recipes brought from their home country. The church also encouraged young people to marry within their ethnic group—a big plus for many parents!

Weddings

Of course, the church was also where marriages took place. A marriage was more than a ceremony with an exchange of rings. It was a chance for the entire community to acknowledge and celebrate the joining of two lives— and have a good time in the process. The wedding goers were more than guests; they were witnesses, and they were also celebrating the joining of two families. In small communities, the two families probably already knew each other. The wedding was yet another of the few chances people had to leave home and join others in a fun time. Weddings were followed by a feast, and very often dancing too.

Weddings were important to the entire community. Wedding licenses were fancy, as shown here, and were often displayed in the couple's home for the rest of their lives as a memory of the happy day.

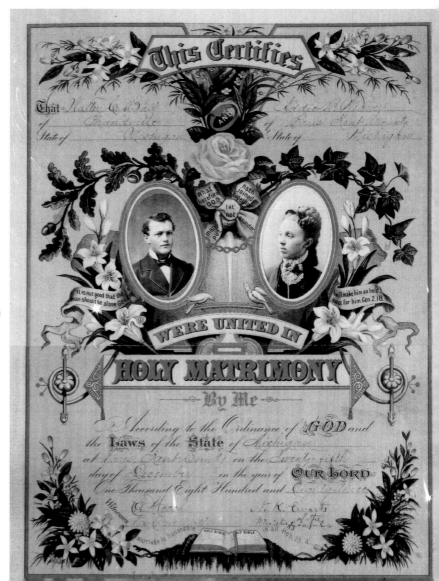

Native American Games

Meanwhile, the people who had already lived in North America when the white settlers arrived, the Native Americans, had their own ways of enjoying themselves. Because in general the Native American lifestyle was more adapted to the outdoors, many of their games featured natural objects and outdoor skills. Perhaps even more than the white settlers in rural America, Native Americans made games of their work. Boys played at warfare and hunting, imitating their fathers in battle or on a hunt. Girls and boys played tag and raced each other during warm weather, and in the winter, the tribes of the north made sleds for their children; in fact, the word "toboggan" is of Algonquin origin.

Games varied from tribe to tribe, from region to region. Tribes of the Plains and Woodlands, where hunting was common, had many games based on hunting skills. Tribes of the Southwest played games involving corn, weather, and grain, while tribes along the Northwest Coast had games that focused on fishing, salmon, and seal. Having no access to ten-cent stores or manufactured toys, Native American children made toys of animal bones, rocks, sticks, leaves, cones, and vines—whatever they could find. They were very creative, inventing toys such as jump-ropes out of leaves and tree fibers. Games that involved stalking quietly or throwing objects as accurately as possible prepared young people to survive.

Hoops like these were used to teach young boys how to aim and shoot arrows. It was fun—but it also helped develop a vital life skill.

Part II
Fun on the Frontier

Generally speaking, the frontier is not usually thought of as a place for light spirits and laughter. Life was hard on the frontier, perhaps harder than any other place in nineteenth-century America. People worked hard; they were often isolated; and many people died. With so much of the day spent working to survive, very little time was left over for fun. And yet, as with other Americans of the 1800s, the settlers found ways to put fun into their work.

The "bee" for instance was largely an invention of the West. Where settlers were so far away from civilization, they tended to come together for work. Just as in rural communities, barn raisings, cabin building, quilt making, and harvests were all good times to come together and enjoy being with one another while work got done.

Reading

Many people don't realize how mentally tiring frontier life could be. Not only was it physically demanding, but it was lonely too, and just plain boring at times. To keep their minds sharp and their spirits from sinking too low, many settlers relied on books. They weren't picky about what they read. Everything from the Bible to months-old newspapers and magazines were fair game for frontier readers.

"Continued stories" or serials were very popular in the West. These thin books came by mail every few weeks and were quickly devoured by Western audiences. Often a settler had to ride half a day to pick up their stories from the mail. The weekly mail was often late, too, and sometimes didn't come at all. Many settlers spent months engrossed in an ongoing story, only to be left hanging forever when the sequel never came in the mail.

Other popular choices were classics in literature, books published by churches, and catalogues like Sears & Roebuck (available in the late 1800s.) Books, magazines, and serials were one way to stay connected to the world back East. They were also a way to stay sane in face of hardship and boredom.

EXTRA! EXTRA!

The news in the nineteenth century could be nearly as exciting as the fictional stories, as this newspaper article demonstrates!

Illustrated Police News
17 Oct 1896

Every seaport as far south as San Diego, and every interior town, and nearly every rancho from the base of the mountains, in which the gold has been found has become suddenly drained of human beings. Americans, Californians, Indians and Sandwich Islanders, men, women and children, indiscriminately. Should there be that success which has repaid the efforts of those employed for the last month, we confess to unhesitatingly believe probably, not only will witness the depopulation of every town, the desertion of every rancho, and the desolation of the once promising crops of the country, but it will also draw largely upon adjacent territories—awake Sonora, and call down upon us, despite her Indian battles, a great many of the good people of Oregon. There are at this time over one thousand souls busied in washing gold, and the yield per diem may be safely estimated at from fifteen to twenty dollars, each individual.

ALARMING EXPERIENCE OF FAIR BATHERS WHO ARE ATTACKED BY AN OCTOPUS.

Holidays

Holidays were important because they offered much needed days of rest and celebration. The Fourth of the July was a big day on the frontier. "Independence Day" was prized by settlers, many of whom had the government (their very own "Uncle Sam") to thank for the free land they'd received.

Christmas remained the most popular holiday. Although it was a day of meager gifts for most children on the frontier, it was a time of great excitement. Even the poorest gift—a doll made from an old pair of socks, for instance—was received with delight, and a single orange was considered to be the best of all gifts. On the plains, settlers often had to find substitutes for the classic pine Christmas tree. They used whatever small trees or shrubs were at hand, including sagebrush.

Christmas trees were not common in the United States until later in the nineteenth century. Even as late as 1851, Henry Schwan, a Cleveland pastor, nearly lost his job because he allowed a tree in his church. In the mid-1850s, President Franklin Pierce put up the first Christmas tree in the White House. On the East Coast, especially in Boston, with its stern Puritan background, schools stayed open on Christmas Day through 1870, and they sometimes expelled students who stayed home. The influx of German and Irish immigrants in the second half of the 1800s brought with them Europe's more joyful Christmas celebrations, and these soon caught on throughout the nation.

In the 1800s, everyone turned out for a Fourth of July celebration.

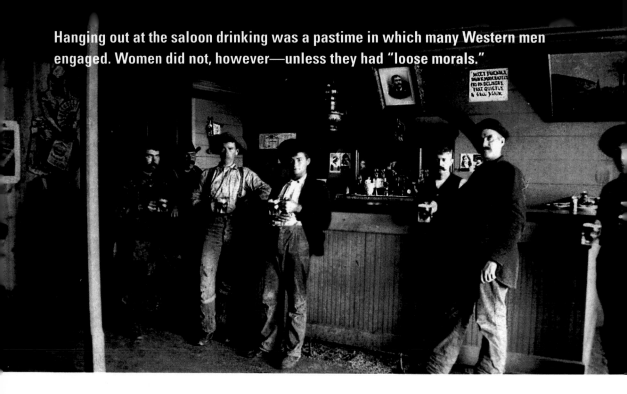

Hanging out at the saloon drinking was a pastime in which many Western men engaged. Women did not, however—unless they had "loose morals."

The "Wild West"

Strong drink, parties ending in fist fights, shoot-outs in the streets: Hollywood and pop culture have exaggerated certain images of the "Wild West." In fact, though, many of the stories of saloon brawling and pistol fighting are true. Everything to do with entertainment in the West tended toward the extreme. What was unique about the West was the enthusiasm and excitement that people brought to social events. With little fun during the average week, settlers were more than ready to let loose when the opportunity arrived.

For men, alcoholic drinks were one way to escape the week's hard work, and the place to drink alcohol was the saloon, which in many cases became the center of social life in a small frontier town. It was also the place where most frowned-upon activities occurred. Card playing and gambling took place there— and there were often prostitutes, too. Prostitutes were called names like "bad women," "ladies of easy virtue," and "soiled doves." The other townspeople generally looked down on them. Even so, in many towns –especially mining or cattle towns where there were lots of single men—prostitution was a thriving business.

Many frontier towns lacked the governmental structure to keep the law. Prostitution was only one of the many dangers of a lawless town. Alcohol and gambling are two pastimes that can lead to violence, and without an effective sheriff to keep peace and arrest offenders, disputes were settled privately, often resulting in unnecessary bloodshed.

Weddings

Even weddings were rougher and rowdier in the West. Westerners had a tradition called a "shivaree" in which they tormented a newlywed couple on the night of their wedding. The shivaree party, composed of the bride and groom's friends, showed up around dusk at the newlywed's house. When the sun finally did set, and they were certain the newlywed couple was in bed, the shivaree party began: banging pots and pans, singing and yelling for the couple's attention. If the groom appeared at the door and offered an acceptable gift—some money or a treat—then the party might go away in peace. But if the gift was unacceptable, or if he refused to answer the door, the party burst into the house, abducted the groom, and carried him miles from home in the dark. It wasn't uncommon for the groom to walk a few miles on his wedding night, often naked or in his underclothes.

One Kansas newspaper editor commented, "It requires backbone to get married out this way."

Singin' and Dancin'

Dances were very popular on the frontier. Whenever a dance was announced, settlers came from far and wide to participate. In the most remote places, a single fiddle player provided the music. Instruments were improvised from whatever was around the house—washboards, spoons, pots, pans. More complicated instruments included the harmonica, guitar, and banjo. Traveling musicians were sometimes invited to play, but for the most part, ordinary people who knew a few tunes took up the task of entertaining the crowd.

Many of the songs they played are songs we still know today: "Skip to My Lou," "Buffalo Gals," and "Home on the Range" were all composed during the late 1800s. Dances were simple, required little or no money, and they could be held in any weather. On winter nights, "cabin dances" were a perfect way to crowd a group of friends and neighbors into a single home and keep warm.

In the 1800s, these two items were necessities for doing your laundry—but they could also be used to improvise percussion backup for a banjo.

SNAPSHOT FROM THE PAST

My name is Liza, Liza Coldwell. I'm fourteen years old, I live in Helena, Montana, and I want to go to a real dance. I'm tired of Presbyterian parties. Mother says the fiddle is the Devil's invention, but I just don't believe her. I've lingered past the Thomas's cabin on my way home some nights, and I can hear the laughter and the lovely music, and it seems harmless to me. But Mother believes the fiddle leads to one place: the bottle. And the bottle, she says, leads to hell. So until I'm married, or until she changes her mind (and that's about as likely as a monsoon here in Montana), I guess I'm stuck with "Presbyterian dances." They've got all the awkwardness of a real dance without any of the fun. We play ring-around-the-rosy, blind man's bluff, and sometimes quote scripture while we weave our hands in and out—never touching hands, of course, just weaving them in and out in a kind of dance routine. And not only is there no fiddle, there's no music at all!

We do manage to have some fun out here in Helena. Everyone hates the winters here because of the bitter cold, but I love them for one reason only, and that's sleigh rides. All summer long I look longingly at the big bob sled sitting uselessly in the grass beside the barn, praying for snow.

Usually we go out sometime in the week before Christmas, provided there's enough snow on the ground. Mother heats rocks up in the stove to put on top of the hay and buffalo blankets that father piles into the sled. When all is ready, Father guides the team of horses. My sister and mother and I just sit in the back, marveling at the warmth and the snow and the darkness. It couldn't be more perfect.

INCREDIBLE INDIVIDUAL
"Buffalo Bill" Cody

In the beginning, Buffalo Bill Cody was known simply as William Frederick Cody. Born to a passionately anti-slavery father, William's early life was filled with danger. His family was always on the run from pro-slavery people angered by his father's speeches. Eventually, they caught up to him. His father died from a stabbing.

The young Bill Cody took to the railroads, looking for any work he could to support his mother. He had a truly "Western" upbringing, working jobs for the railroad, the gold-mines of Colorado, and even the Pony Express at one point. Eventually, however, he found the job that would give him his name: buffalo hunting. The story goes that Bill Cody earned the title "Buffalo Bill" when he killed 4,860 buffalo in eight months.

His fame came later. Over the years, Bill acquired skills and a certain familiarity with the West and many of its famous inhabitants. He used his connections to create what would become one of the most well known shows in the world: "Buffalo Bill's Wild West." The show began in the early 1880s, in Nebraska, and acted like a traveling circus. Bill assembled a mixed group of Western characters. There were midget cowboys, sharpshooters such as Annie Oakley, and even famous Native Americans such as Sitting Bull. Bill found Turks, Arabs, Mongols, and other exotic figures that amazed American audiences. Much of the show was acted out like a play, with Indian attacks on carriages being "recreated" before audiences who held their breath. Typically, the show ended with a "reenactment" of Custer's Last Stand. A showman to the end, Bill himself played the role of General Custer.

The Wild West show toured all over America and Europe for over thirty years. It is many ways responsible for many of the stereotypes and misconceptions of the American West in the imaginations of both Americans and foreigners. Even so, it inspired generations of people to learn more about the "true" West, and the real stories of how the West was won. Despite the fact that he cast Indians in the role of attackers in many of his shows, Bill worked hard to introduce white people to the true character of Native Americans. He encouraged Indian performers in his show to bring their families on tour as a way to show white audiences that Indians were people too, people with a very different culture but who had families just like theirs own. Bill once said, "Every Indian outbreak that I have ever known has resulted from broken promises and broken treaties by the government."

Despite his namesake and reputation for killing bison, Bill actually supported conservation. He spoke out against hide-hunting and supported a hunting season. He knew the West and loved it. He wanted to see the many wonders of his lifetime remain a part of American culture forever.

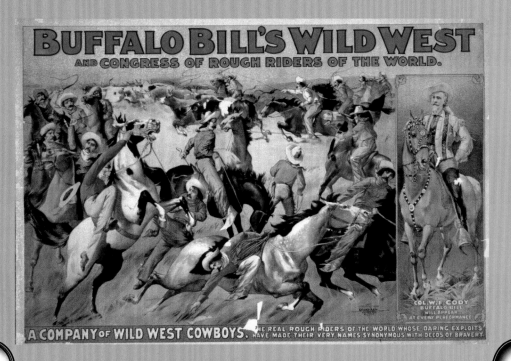

EYEWITNESS ACCOUNT

A Letter from Buffalo Bill Cody to Colonel William Ray, August 1887

My Dear Colonel,

It was a pleasant surprise to receive your letter. I have often thought of you and wondered what had become of you. So you are still on top of the earth? Well, ever since I got out of the mudhole in New Orleans, things have been coming my way pretty smooth and I have captured this country, from the queen down. I am doing them to the tune of $10,000 a day. Talk about show business! There never was anything like it ever known and never will be again, and with my European reputation, you can easily guess the business I will do when I get back to my own country. Its pretty hard work with two and three performances a day and the society racket at reception dinners, etc. No man—even Grant —was received better than your humble servant. I have dined with every one of the royalty, from Albert, Prince of Wales down. I sometimes wonder if it is the same old Bill Cody, the bull-wacker. Well, colonel, I still wear the same sized hat, and when I make my pile I am coming back to visit all the old boys. If you meet any of them tell them I ain't got the big head worth a cent. I am over here for dust. Will be glad to hear from any of them. Write me again.

Your old time friend,

BILL CODY.

Buffalo Bill Cody with his show.

Part III
The Sights and Sounds of a New Era

Rise of Urban America

As people continued to move toward the cities and as immigrants poured into American streets, the great American experiment with democracy was put to the test: how could so many people, from so many different cultures, get along?

Entertainment was one way America found to answer that question. The technological marvels of the World's Fair, the many traveling circuses, and magic shows, even the very architecture of the rising cities—they allowed Americans from all backgrounds to laugh, sigh, "ooh," and "ah" as equals.

By the 1800s, New York City had become a busy urban center, with immigrants sailing there from all around the world.

The World's Fair was held in Chicago in 1893. People from all over the country flocked there to be amazed by the modern technology that was displayed.

African-American Influence

Many of the trademarks of American culture in the late 1800s were the result of African-Americans entering society as free people. With the fall of slavery during the Civil War, an enormous population was added to America's public. African Americans worked hard—but they also knew how to have a good time.

When Africans first came to North America, they brought along their many and varied cultures. Africa is an enormous continent, and there was no single "African" society. People who came from central and western Africa represented different nations, tribes, and peoples, all with their own songs, histories, and dances.

As slaves, African Americans created their own rich culture, but they had few opportunities to buy goods or shape the larger culture around them. As free people, however, their tastes and influence began to be felt in a new way throughout America.

"Minstrel shows" were places where white people would go to enjoy black talent.

But circumstances changed when they arrived in America, where many different cultures were forced to live under the same slaveholder's roof. Over time, as Africans became African Americans, a unique culture emerged with an identity all its own. African American dances were one expression of this cultural melting pot.

Take the "cake walk," for example, a dance almost impossible to describe, a mixture of wild gestures and formal movements. Although no one is certain exactly where it began, most historians agree it was a form of dance used by slaves to mock the formal dances of their white owners. It takes the stiff, rigid European style so popular at wealthy parties in the South and makes it look downright silly and fun. Pretty soon, white people were dancing it too.

Ragtime

The cake walk prepared the way for another wild mix of styles—this time musical styles—called "ragtime." Ragtime became an almost instant American sensation in the 1890s. It was an African American creation that combined African syncopation (a term for certain kinds of off-beat rhythms) and European classical music, especially marches. By far the most popular composer of ragtime songs (called "rags") was Scott Joplin, a black man who almost singlehandedly made the genre popular.

In those days, before the phonograph or other forms of recorded music were widespread, songs were shared through sheet music. Amateur and professional musicians alike could buy Joplin's rags and bring the new sound into their neighborhood restaurant or the living room of their home.

Ragtime and other musical creations of the late 1800s set the stage for musical revolutions to come, including jazz. The new sounds of the 1880s and 1890s were a step away from traditional folk songs and hymns sung by ordinary people. This was a new form of popular music that was as much style as melody. It was a new way of making music—and listeners couldn't get enough of it!

Sheet music from the late 1800s shows how popular ragtime had become. Many white people might still be guilty of racism—but at the same time, they couldn't help but enjoy the music African Americans had brought to the nation.

INCREDIBLE INDIVIDUAL
Scott Joplin

Scott Joplin, the "King of Ragtime" music, was born in Texas in 1868. Even when he was a little boy, Scott had an extraordinary musical talent. His parents encouraged him, and by the time he was eleven he was already skilled on the banjo, and he was beginning to play the piano. As a teenager, he worked as a dance musician.

He traveled around the Southern states of America as an itinerant musician, and went to Chicago just as ragtime became a national craze after the World's Fair of 1897. His composition in 1899 of the "Maple Leaf Rag" brought him fame, and the song had a profound influence on the music world. It also brought Scott a steady income for life with royalties of one cent per sale. During his lifetime, Joplin did not reach this level of success again, and he frequently had financial problems,

Although Joplin's music was popular, he did not receive recognition as a serious composer for more than fifty years after his death. Then, in 1973, his music was featured in the motion picture, "The Sting", which won and Academy Award for its film score. Three years later, in 1976, nearly sixty years after his death, Joplin's opera "Treemonisha" won the Pulitzer Prize.

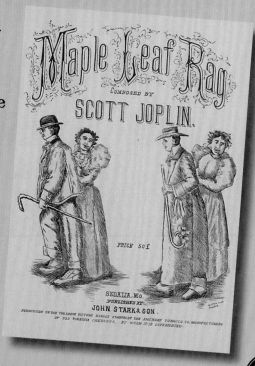

EXTRA! EXTRA!

Not everyone was excited about ragtime and cakewalks, as this newspaper article reveals:

Cleveland Gazette, 1893

According to our Circleville, Ohio, correspondence, published elsewhere in this paper, the pastor of the A.M.E. church of that place so far forgot himself as to permit a "CAKE WALK" to be held in the CHURCH. The presiding elder of that district and bishop, also, ought to have an interview with the pastor at once. "Cake walk" are disgraceful relics of slavery days and should not be tolerated for a moment in intelligent Afro-American COMMUNITIES to say nothing of CHURCHES.

Singing 'Round the Piano

At the end of the 1800s, not all music was ragtime, of course. People liked songs with simple melodies as well, songs that were easy to sing in groups.

When people got together to sing, they often did so around a piano. As the middle class grew towards the end of the 1800s, so did the demand for pianos in the home. Manufacturers were happy to oblige the public, and companies sprung up around the United States to mass-produce pianos for middle- and upper-class families.

Often the sheet music for popular tunes was sold in the form of "piano rolls" for player pianos. The player piano is one of the earliest links in the long line of technology to record and play music. In many ways, believe it or not, the player piano is an ancestor to the stereo and the iPod! The idea of a piano that plays its own music took hold in the 1870s and was popularized in the 1890s.

Playing the piano was something children enjoyed as much as adults, and girls were especially likely to have lessons to teach them this pleasurable activity.

The inner works of a player piano.

The technology was much like an enormous music box, using barrels and pins and a pressure system to play the long rolls of sheet music filled with tiny holes. In the early days of the player piano, someone had to sit at the bench and carefully pump two peddles that kept the sheet music rolling through the piano at the correct tempo (or speed). Eventually, even this was made unnec-essary when electricity started being used to power the pedals. Then all a person had to do was load the music, start the system, and sit back and enjoy.

Rolls like this made the music in a player piano, a little like enormous music boxes.

The Greatest Show on Earth

Almost nothing was as exciting to Americans as the circuses that traveled the country in the second half of the 1800s.

Circuses were not just opportunities to see exotic animals or watch acrobats perform high-flying feats. Entering the circus was like entering an alternate universe. The circus was a place where women had beards, midgets served drinks, and strange animals such as the famed "Feejee Mermaid" could be found. (The "mermaid" was actually a monkey torso sewn to a fish tail!) Circuses were part performance, part illusion, and they were always competing with one another for bigger audiences. Many of the exhibits in early circuses have been discontinued today, as people realized the inhumane things being done to both humans and animals.

WONDERFUL PERFORMING GEESE, ROOSTERS AND MUSICAL DONKEY.

As is still the tradition today, circuses traveled from place to place, attracting eager audiences at every turn. Before the circus became popular in America, it was traditionally something of a comedy show. It had clowns, comedians with funny dialogues, some jugglers, and a few well-trained horses. But the new American circus of the nineteenth century made everything bigger, more spectacular, and more dangerous. Animal tamers walked into cages with lions and leopards, trapeze artists swung by their legs hundreds of feet in the air, and "fire breathers" walked about spitting flames from their mouths.

The circus was as popular in the American West as it was in the cities of the East. P.T. Barnum, one of the earliest heroes of the American circus, developed special railroad cars to transport his show across the country. Imagine railroad cars full of trained zebras, elephants, and musical donkeys! Barnum successfully merged his circus with several smaller circuses, at each turn making his show grander and more spectacular. After all, as a circus' reputation as the "greatest in the world" grew, so did its ticket sales.

The caption on this Barnum & Bailey poster reads, "L'Auto Bolide thrilling dip of death. M'lle Mauricia de Tiers, the fearless, young and fascinating Parisian, in a dreadful, headlong leap, loop and topsy turvy plunging somersault with an automobile. The sensation of all sensations, which may be aptly termed a fearful frolic with fate. An absolutely unparalleled deed of daring, just as illustrated and costing nearly $2,000.00 a minute. The most expensive, as well as the most hazardous act ever devised."

On Easter Sunday in 1882, thousands gathered at a New York City dock to watch Barnum unload his latest addition from Africa: an enormous elephant he would name "Jumbo." Sadly, the elephant only lasted three years in the circus before being hit by a freight train. But even then, Barnum could not be stopped: he had Jumbo's remains (his giant hide and skeleton) put on display in his circus.

Reputation is what drove Barnum to continually seek out new sights and new wonders for his circus. There were some advantages to making circuses bigger. For years, smaller circuses preyed on small-town audiences, promising spectacles and charging high prices but failing to deliver anything but a bunch of bad tricks. Showmen like P.T. Barnum and the Ringling Brothers used their money and power to create shows truly worthy of their reputation.

INCREDIBLE INDIVIDUAL
P.T. Barnum

"There's a sucker born every minute," is a phrase often credited to P. T. Barnum (1810–1891), one of the greatest of all American showmen. Barnum may not have actually been the one to say this, but his reputation was often built on the fact that there are (and always will be) a lot of gullible people in the world!

Phineas Taylor Barnum was a businessman, and entertainer, remembered for promoting celebrated hoaxes and for founding the circus that became the Ringling Bros. and Barnum & Bailey Circus. His successes may have made him the first "show business" millionaire.

Born in Bethel, Connecticut, Barnum became a small-business owner in his early twenties, and founded a weekly paper, The Herald of Freedom, in Danbury in 1829. He moved to New York City in 1834, where he embarked on an entertainment career with a variety troupe called "Barnum's Grand Scientific and Musical Theater." Soon after this, he bought Scudder's American Museum, which he renamed after himself and used as a site to promote hoaxes and human curiosities such as the "Feejee mermaid" and "General Tom Thumb." By late 1846, Barnum's Museum was drawing 400,000 visitors a year.

But Barnum was not only an entertainer. He was also an author, publisher, philanthropist, and even a politician—and like a rubber ball, he never seemed to stop bouncing! After a series of financial disasters, he recovered and started a lecture tour, mostly as a temperance speaker (lecturing about the evils of alcohol), and by 1860, he emerged from debt and built a mansion he named Lindencroft. Around the same time, his museum added America's first aquarium and expanded its wax figure department. While he claimed that "politics were always distasteful to me," he was elected to the Connecticut legislature in 1865 as a Republican for Fairfield, and served two terms.

Barnum also spoke up on behalf of African Americans. He stood before Congress and said, "A human soul is not to be trifled with. It may inhabit the body of a Chinaman, a Turk, an Arab or a Hotentot—it is still an immortal spirit!" In 1875, Barnum was mayor of Bridgeport, Connecticut, for a year, where he worked to improve the water supply, bring gas lighting to streets, and enforcing liquor and prostitution laws. He helped start the Bridgeport Hospital in 1878 and was its first president.

In his sixties, Barnum was still going strong. At sixty-one, he established "P. T. Barnum's Grand Traveling Museum, Menagerie, Caravan & Hippodrome," a traveling circus, menagerie, and museum of "freaks," which billed itself as "The Greatest Show on Earth." Barnum was the first to move his circus by train. Given the lack of paved highways in America, this turned out to be a shrewd business move that enlarged Barnum's market.

P.T. Barnum changed the way Americans had a good time. Nearly singlehandedly, he convinced the nation that theaters could be places to be educated and delighted, respectable family entertainment rather than "dens of evil." He started the nation's first matinees to encourage families to attend and to lessen the fear of crime. He also organized flower shows, beauty contests, dog shows, poultry contests, and (most popular of all) baby contests (for fattest baby, handsomest twins, etc.). In the end, he said of himself, "I am a showman by profession . . . and all the gilding shall make nothing else of me."

Zoos

The Central Park Zoo opened in 1864, the first to open in the United States. (The Philadelphia zoo was founded in 1859, but because of the Civil War, it didn't open its gates until 1874.) At first, the concept of a zoo was still strange to most people. In fact, the Central Park Zoo originally began as the Central Park Menagerie. It was more a collection of exotic animals given as gifts from all over the world.

Zoos became yet another way a city could flaunt its wealth and build its reputation. Walking through a zoo was like traveling to other worlds. In the days before photography became widespread, many people had never seen anything but illustrations of these exotic creatures. When given the amazing opportunity to see them

The earliest zoos were simply menageries, collections of animals in small cages.

up close, Americans leaped at the chance. Some early animals at the Central Park Zoo included swans and a bear, and by turn of the century the zoo even had an elephant.

Magicians Amaze

Magic (or the art of illusion) has been around for a very long time. During the centuries leading up to the 1800s, many magicians earned their living by doing small shows on street corners, or performing for a royal court. All that changed in the 1800s, when magicians took their acts to the next level.

Magicians we still remember today were immensely famous in their own time. Harry Houdini, considered one of the best magicians in history, was known on almost every continent in his lifetime. Magicians were showmen as much as they were illusionists. They were always trying to make their shows bigger, more dangerous, and more unforgettable.

Harry Houdini was a master escape artist who thrilled and delighted his audiences.

Harry Houdini, in a packing case said to contain six hundred pounds of iron weights, is shown here being lowered into New York Bay. He is credited with having escaped in two minutes and fifty-five seconds.

Houdini made himself famous by doing incredible escapes. He handcuffed himself, buried himself, and dunked himself underwater—and always escaped. Other magicians such as Harry Kellar stuck to more traditional stage shows; some of Kellar's most famous illusions included a "floating-head" trick, in which Kellar sat in a chair on stage while his head appeared to detach and float about the room. Another of his illusions was the called "the levitation of Princess Karnac" in which he raised a young girl's body fully off the floor.

Shopping and "The Ladies' Mile"

As cities and household incomes grew, so did the demand for places to shop. The customers were mostly women, leading to shopping districts such as the one in New York City to be called the "Ladies' Mile"—but it wasn't uncommon for a man and wife to spend a day shopping for the entire family.

New York City, Philadelphia, and Chicago led the way when it came to long stretches of shops. Macy's Department Store opened on the "Ladies' Mile" in New York City, considered by many at the time to be the best shopping district in the United States. In Chicago, Marshal Field opened his own department store, Marshall Field's, on State Street.

The owners of these enormous stores spent huge sums to make their buildings inviting. They built beautiful staircases, raised glass ceilings, and decorated everything to appear rich and lavish. Even those who could only afford to look, not buy, enjoyed a day at the department store. The stores were as much about experiencing wealth as they were about spending money.

By the end of the century, Americans' simple pleasures were starting to disappear. More and more, the

At the end of the 1800s, people enjoyed walking the streets and shopping as a way to pass the time.

City parks were places where people could congregate on a Saturday afternoon and stroll around.

Public transportation gave people new freedom, and even young girls could venture out on shopping outings.

United States would become a nation that paid money for its pleasure. Entertainment would soon become one of its biggest and most profitable businesses. Still, we've never really forgotten those long-ago fun-filled days of the nineteenth century. Informal baseball games, playing board games, and singing songs together are still as much fun as they ever were!

Think About It

You've read about how important it was for people everywhere to find ways to have fun and entertain themselves in the 1800s.

- Why was entertainment such an important part of life in the 1800s?

- Is it more or less important to people like us in the 21st century?

- What do you think the future of entertainment in America will be like?

In the 1800s, people in rural America and on the frontier often combined work and play, coming together as a community to get a big job done (such as raising a barn or husking hundreds of bushels of corn) while enjoying the company of their neighbors and socializing.

- Do people still try to combine having fun with getting a big job done?

- Think of some examples in your own community.

- Why do you think this way of doing things can be successful?

Words Used in This Book

distractions: Amusing things that can help take your mind off serious matters.

exotic: Unusual, mysterious things from faraway places.

genre: A particular style of literature or art.

gullible: Easy to fool and take advantage of.

influx: The arrival of a large group.

itinerant: Traveling from place to place in order to make a living.

mass-produce: To manufacture a product in large numbers, cheaply and efficiently.

relics: The remnants and remains of the past.

royalties: Money earned by an author for the sale of a book, piece of music, etc, based on the number of copies sold.

sensation: Something that becomes very, very popular, usually very quickly.

technological: Having to do with advances in machinery and industry.

variety troupe: A group of entertainers that performs a wide range of acts, including singing, dancing, and comedy.

Find Out More

In Books

McComb, David. *Spare Time in Texas: Recreation and History in the Lone Star State*. Austin, Tex.: University of Texas Press, 2008.

Rumble, Victoria R. *Outdoor Recreation and Leisure in 19th Century America*. Florence, Ala.: Thistledew Books, 2009.

On the Internet

Church Socials
www.materialreligion.org/journal/potluck.html

Nebraska Government Corn Husking History
www.nebraskahistory.org/publish/publicat/timeline/corn_husking.htm

PBS "Frontier Experience"
www.pbs.org/wnet/frontierhouse/project/index.html

The Player Piano's History
www.pianoworld.com/player.htm

The websites listed on this page were active at the time of publication. The publisher is not responsible for websites that have changed their address or discontinued operation since the date of publication. The publisher will review and update the websites upon each reprint.

Index

Picture Credits

American Folk Art Museum: p. 19
Berger Collection: pp. 16–17
Creative Commons: pp. 32, 34, 36
Dover: pp. 54–55
Goodyear Archival Collection: pp. 37, 38, 39
Granger Collection: pp. 52–53
Johnson, Jonathan Eastman: pp. 14–15,
Library of Congress: pp. 14–15, 18, 20–21, 22–23, 28–29, 30–31, 33, 35, 41, 48–49, 50–51, 52, 54–55, 56–57, 58–59
National Institute of American History: p. 24
Renoir, Pierre Auguste; Creative Commons: p. 47
Walker, Tim; Creative Commons: p. 47

About the Author and the Consultant

Zachary Chastain is an independent writer and actor living in Binghamton, New York. He is the author of various educational books for both younger and older audiences.

John Gillis is a Rutgers University Professor of History Emeritus. A graduate of Amherst College and Stanford University, he has taught at Stanford, Princeton, University of California at Berkeley, as well as Rutgers. Gillis is well known for his work in social history, including pioneering studies of age relations, marriage, and family. The author or editor of ten books, he has also been a fellow at both St. Antony's College, Oxford, and Clare Hall, Cambridge.